The Nostalgia Collection

Jackie Smith

A catalogue record for this book is available from the National Library of Australia

Copyright © 2021 Jackie Smith

All rights reserved. No part of this publication may be reproduced, stored in a retrieval system, or transmitted in any form or by any means, electronic, mechanical, photocopying, recording or otherwise without prior permission of the author.

Publisher:
Inspiring Publishers
P.O. Box 159, Calwell, ACT Australia 2905
Email: publishaspg@gmail.com
http://www.inspiringpublishers.com

National Library of Australia Cataloguing-in-Publication entry

Author: Smith, Jackie

Title: **The Nostalgia Collection**/*Jackie Smith*

ISBN: 978-1-922618-02-3 (Print)
　　　978-1-922618-03-0 (eBook)

When not writing poetry, Jackie Smith is a freelance journalist, editor and proof-reader and marketing graduate based in Brisbane, QLD, Australia. Her articles have been published through a variety of local and national media outlets, and she has had success publishing poetry and short stories in various anthologies. *The Nostalgia Collection* is her first full-length book.

Connect with her online via the following channels:

Blog: jackiesmithwrites.wordpress.com
Facebook: facebook.com/jackiesmithwrites
Twitter: twitter.com/jasmith_89
Instagram: instagram.com/jackiesmithwrites

Dedicated to Nan and Pa,

May you forever be in my heart.

table of Contents

New Dawn 11

My Lonely Soldier (Ode to the Firefighter) 12

Little Blue Bird 13

Daredevil 15

Tomorrow, My Friend, Until Tomorrow 16

Anti-Gravity 18

Bystander 19

Atlantis (The Siren's Call) 20

A Toast, I Declare, to a Life Worth Living 21

Heartbreak's Anthem 22

Snake Goddess 23

Emotions 24

Goodbye 25

My Procrastination 26

Aftermath 27

Milky Way 28

Survival 29

Haze 30

Reality (Fantasy) 31

Magic in the Morning 32

Demon..34

Options..35

The Ringmaster...36

Edit Me..37

Depression I (Galaxy)...38

Depression II (Black Hole).................................39

Depression III (Kaleidoscope)............................40

Disciple 41

Begin...42

Compass 43

Remind me.. 44

Mama..45

Promise...46

Heartbreak & Freedom 47

As it All Goes Black 48

Rainbow..49

Stand and Cry...50

Trapped..51

Of Love 52

Wildflowers...53

You..54

Believe 55

Fake (The Waltz)...56

Evil Surrenders 57
Hide and Seek (A Game) 58
Minutes 59
Sleeping Under Windowpanes 60
Please 61
Bruises 62
Follow Me 63
Dreams 64
Talk to Me 65
Serenity 66
Choke 67
The Theory of Colour 68
Ancient Chapters (Red Herrings) 69
Ambition 70
Perspective 71
Down 72
Labyrinth 73
Unknown 74
Innocence 75
In the Looking Glass 76
Home Truths and a Long Winding Road 77
Communication Breakdown 78
Held Captive 79

Nature 80

Peace 81

Escape 82

Someday 83

Poetry in Motion 84

Nostalgia 85

Home 86

The Fires 87

Riot 88

Why? 89

Drowning 90

Dancer 91

Stalker 92

Midnight Conversations (Sleeping Dogs Lie) 93

Prisoner 94

I've Been Thinking 95

Sorry for Your Loss 96

Isolation 97

Destiny in Black and White 98

Note: *Bruises* and *Destiny in Black and White* were first published via competitions run by Write4Fun in Australia.

New Dawn

If we ran out of oxygen,
Would the world just choke?
Stop dead on the spot, forever suspended in uncharted galaxies,
Where time and space cease to exist.

Would we become distant pinpricks of light,
Death stars viewed from miles away, glowing in a night sky
Reflecting the red dirt of Mars' surface,
Fossils to be discovered by some ancient species who have not yet welcomed their first generation.

Would we all just shatter, splinter and crack like glass
too fragile for the heavy weight of the world descended into chaos.

Or could we, in fact, become the light in someone's darkness,
a flickering candle to show the way,
an element of peace and prosperity,
passion, endurance,
and the beginning of a new dawn.

My Lonely Soldier (Ode to the Firefighter)

Smouldering cinders choke our airways,
Remnants of fire still burning
Weep, weary one
Lay your head next to mine.
Wrap your arms around me
Reassuring and strong.

I will comfort you
Leaving the rest of the world behind
Until dawn turns into day
And the fire's embers fade
Into a nothingness
Upon which we will
Build again.

Little Blue Bird

Little blue bird, leave here and escape.
Run from all this torture and pain,
For it is your turn to fly,
And you are no longer needed
Here today.

So fly away, be free and alone
Be gone, for you are no longer
A part of us. You have already left our hearts.

Several days have passed and you have left
But not returned to this place where you should be.
This place where you belong.

Oh, come back, little blue bird. We miss you so.
We miss your laughter and your tears.
We miss the things you used to say
That made us laugh.
Hysterical Laughter.

Those things are still said,
But no one told us how they would make us cry
Hysterical tears
Because your voice did not tell us
And we can't hear your laughter,
Laughing with us.

Daredevil

I walk the tightrope,
Just to see how far I'd fall,
Cross the road when the light is red,
to play chicken with machines much heavier than me.

I fly a kite just to watch it rise,
letting go of the string.
I hide in shadows
to listen to secrets
I do not want to hear,
Touch my hand to the flame,
even though I know it will burn.

I curse the day I met you,
yet revel in our shared memory.

Tomorrow, My Friend, Until Tomorrow

Death is not something to be feared
So I shall not,
cannot,
must not
Weep! as you are drawn further
Away from me.

I am left here
In the Dark
For the last candle has
Long since burnt out; an end to your beautiful life.

Help!
Try as I might to banish
Them, tears flow freely
I cannot speak.

As the last song plays
And I sing along in chorus
A song that most reminds
Me of You,

The last rose petal has
Fallen
And I go on to live
Another Day.
May your spirit finally
Be Free.

Anti-Gravity

Gravity is not my friend;
It cuts me like a knife.
We meet frequently on the battlefield
at dawn,
not far from Newton's apple tree.

We battle for purchase on unceded land,
it's force strong enough to knock me off-balance,
but too weak to keep me upright.

This branch does not bend,
It breaks,
Succumbing to invisible barriers it cannot sustain.
But out there,

In space,
I take comfort in the knowledge that I will one day be weightless,
Light as a feather, stardust, a memory whose impression will forever
LIVE ON.

Bystander

I have my father's eyes,
my father's evil eyes.
My face is not my own
It is hers, my mother's,
the make-up of Hell.

I tried to explain to you
But you didn't listen
To hear
The words that I speak
To tell you that
To live is a veil
Hiding the vile soul
Of evil.
And I am delivered from evil's carnation
The petals as they fall drop blood on my heart.
Fingers like knives pierce my spirit.
But you didn't hear my scream.
So I don't know what to do
And I have no one to love.

Atlantis (The Siren's Call)

I hear it before I see it
Thoughts like waves,
In the whirlpool of your mind
Hearts beating in time
To the howl of the wind.
Salt air fills my lungs, its perfume
so strong I can
Taste it on my
tongue.
We breathe
          DEEP ...
The setting sun throws pink hues
Across the ocean's surface
so clear and true we can almost
see dolphins play
in seabeds,
frolicking and weaving through seaweed
in search of Atlantis,
or other secret worlds.

A Toast, I Declare, to a Life Worth Living

The flame flickered.
For a moment so brief
I saw you.
Maybe it wasn't even real.
It could have just been a trick of the eyes,
An illusion.
But it was enough to make me
Stand and walk on
Toward the horizon of a new day and
The everlasting sun.
A toast, I declare, to a life worth living.

Heartbreak's Anthem

You shot the gun that brought down cupid's arrow
Love lost with a bullet, gunpowder residue on hands.
I watched from violet blue shadows as you fled the scene
of heartbreak and broken wings.

Desperate thoughts give way to desperate actions.
Covered your eyes to hide evidence of your crime.
Splintered shards of shattered hearts leaving drops of
blood in your wake.
The night bruises the sky, a painter who has run out of
colour,
because
LOVE IS DEAD.

This nightmare trembles in the waking
Distant thunderstorms dance gleefully on distant shores,
And as I lay my head upon the pillow I realise,
There is no one to blame,
And the monsters that are outside my window,
Lurk within me.

Snake Goddess

Roses drip petals
like blood from pricked fingertips.

Serpents for hair,
My heart is a stone unfractured
Rallying against your war-cry.

In the trauma of my memory,
Long forgotten by Athena's curse,
I shatter
into a million pieces
so fine that you'll never put me
back
together
again.

Emotions

A child laughs, made happy by the slightest thing.
A balloon floats away, driven by the wind ...
A child cries.
Sweets...
Troubles and woes forgotten.
A promise...
Hopeful dreams.
Innocence...
What does it mean?

Goodbye

If I knew then that day would be our last,
the things I always meant to say would no longer be unsaid.

As the sun became a silhouette, I'd whisper how much I love you,
how you are the brightest star in all our constellation,
how the timbre of your voice is like a lullaby on the nights when I can't sleep,
shared memories play like a movie that reminds me of better days,
when your skin was not paper thin against the grey light.
If I knew then, that today would be our last,
I'd ask you to tell me all your stories,
just so that I didn't have to tell this one about how much I regret what I was too scared to say.
Goodbye.

My Procrastination

Your fingertips tell me
That you are ready, that it is almost time
As they grasp my hand a little tighter
Every time I see you.

The crack in your voice
Through the phone line, tells me
You are getting older
But are prepared
To meet your fate.

But I'm not.
I can't allow that.
So when I pull away
From your tender touch
It is not that I
Don't love you

I love you too much to let you go.

Aftermath

Your tongue lashed me
In your pale shades of blue and grey.

You should have trusted me
Loved me
Wanted me
Believed in me enough
To share yourself.

Now life after you is just
A blurry mess
Visions of psychedelic colours
I cannot see,
Or even want to because
There is no
You and me.

Milky Way

Tell me I'm kaleidoscope dreaming,
all hail the golden moon.
I walk the sunsets,
follow the dawn
dance til twilight envelops me
in its reverie.

Damaged stars shatter in a shimmering light,
sparking the sky with diamonds,
born from inky coal and
abandoned promises.

I don't know if I believe in your God,
a celestial being unproven by scientists,
but I do believe in light.
I've seen its power,
the way it calls in the shadow
of darkness,
like a candle burning its flame.

Survival

They say
Sticks and Stones
May break my Bones
But names will never
Hurt me.

They say
What doesn't
Kill you
Makes you
Stronger.

They say
There is a Light
At the End of the tunnel.

So I have to keep
Trudging along
Like Nothing's wrong
And pretend to believe
In Rainbows and Santa.

Haze

To cry a million tears would be to feel relief.
Even just for a moment or two,
And remember when this wasn't about me and you
But rather a bigger picture that I
can't yet see.
A vision of uncertainty.

Reality (Fantasy)

Children work busily
Without a sound
Uncomfortable, lonely
Bones aching as they try to
Stretch weary muscles.
This is their life and here they live it.

A conveyer belt of monotony
Dawn til dusk, no break
Dirty feet, dirty hands
Disease at every turn
All for the promise of twenty cents at the
End of the day (end of their life).

Skin and bones, a girl works tirelessly,
Wishing on a long-forgotten star
For a future where she lives and laughs
And loves (anywhere but here ...)
But deep down she knows,
Nothing will come of her dreams
(Thinking, 'This is where I belong.')

Magic in the Morning

I.
Loneliness etches slowly across
the dark night sky
as static echoes nightmares I would rather forget.

Starbursts fall in the world around me,
yet I am blind to their light.
Can't relish in the delight of your wonder,
only see the ashes in the flame.

Satellites cascade in the darkness,
searching for a new truth,
an embodiment, an entity
anything to hold on to
and stabilise if only for a minute,
if only for a second
until balance restores.

II.

Magic in the morning
A glittering dazzling glow.
Kaleidoscope memory shines,
A smile in the darkness,
Burning like a candle
Warm like a fire
Encompassing me with love,
Sparks of brilliance,
Of reverie.
Because when we're all happy,
How could I ever be sad?

Demon

After Seb McKinnon's illustrations *Sower of the Temptation* and *Enchanted Evening*

Dancing upon the rippling waves,
she calls from nightmares unbound
howling to the moon of
lost sorrows
A quarter past midnight
and a minute too late.

Her shrouded beauty remains
a mystery
as she lights the way for
withered disciples
to follow
all crimson robes and
empathy
while we sink further into dreamscapes
foretold by myth and legend
the truth-sayers deny on a moonlit morning.

Options

Take a look.
What do you see?
Do you see me?
Am I but a shadow of my former self?
Bleeding, breathing and sneaking around
Haunting you until the day you die
Because it is my duty and
I have no other choice.

Naivety is a strange thing.
It creeps upon you
Like a monster
Under the bed.

The Ringmaster

Broken mirrors reflect broken souls,
Revealing cracks hidden from a world unchanged by years of shattered dreams.
Seven years bad luck.
Prick your finger on splintered glass,
Blood pooling on concrete surface,
as lightbulbs buzz overhead, tropical hibiscus hues splayed across faces made up for audience's pleasure.
As the ringmaster hypes a crowd unfamiliar with your ghosts.

So you take the stage, spotlight blinding
Night so dark it spills across the sky like ink.
We paint the smile for all to see,
Happy faces
Because if the map is not a territory,
And all we know is not true
How will we ever tell lies from reality,
If a silhouette cannot be seen among shadows,
does that mean it no longer exists?

Edit Me

Edit me,
I need to be proofread.

I do not
Fit
Into your stereotype
Your mould
And even if I did
I would struggle against
The bonds that
Tie me down
To your set ways.

Because this is not your story
It is mine.
And you have no right to
Tamper with my life.

Depression I (Galaxy)

Out there, it's a world of break ups and love affairs
I want to see beyond the black hole
That draws me into its pit
Deep and dark.

In this endless universe
I feel forgotten, like Pluto.
As the planets align
I am uninvited
Sinking into the oblivion of my own
Isolation.

I want to break free
To look forward to times
Beyond the rainbow
And not get caught up
In the atmosphere of
My thoughts.

Depression II (Black Hole)

This black hole draws me in
The starry, starry night
Once so bright splutters
And fades into dull lifelessness.

My life haunts me as I struggle
Against bonds to muster words
Unfurling my emotions.

With no compass and
A darkened sun
To guide me to a
Galaxy of happiness.

Am I to be lost forever?

Depression III (Kaleidoscope)

Red, red light
    Transcends into purple
    With a hint of blue
            Defiant indigo.

Sunny, sunny days
    Tell of smiles and ways
    Thoughts and visions of brighter times
            Inhale, Exhale.

Acid tears fall
    For unexplainable reasons
    Indefensible voices
    Crowd my brain
    Saying unexplainable things.

Disciple

If you were a galaxy far away
Stars burning brightly,
Constellations playing dot to dot with meteorites and asteroids,
I'd lose myself in your stars as the sun sets,
fly in a rocket ship to witness Earth's orbit from your perspective,
lasso your moon to bring you closer to me.

I'd walk the no-name streets of your poorest towns,
Cart water for your dying.
I'd follow your map to nowhere,
And beyond.

If you were a galaxy far away,
I'd be your satellite,
guided by your every move,
And forever igniting the way home.

Begin

I dream of a place
Bigger than
Here
With lots of traffic
Where no one knows my name,
And I can begin my life.

But would I survive
When in this little corner
Of the world,
A place I can call
My Own
And a life
Barely beginning,
I can hardly
Tie my shoes
Or button my clothes.

Compass

I wandered into this dreamland
Following misleading stop signs
Skipping along a rainbow path
In search of an Almighty Force
To guide me on my way.

It does not come but I shall wait
Til the sun creeps
Towards the horizon
And merges with the moon.
Eclipse, silence
Perfection.

Remind me

Remind me of a time before
Shotgun in hand,
You stood on bloodstained carpets,
Eyes crazy, unseeing.

When violence wasn't the autoreply to
Answers you didn't want to hear.

Remind me of those honey-soaked days
Indian summer
When we used to walk along the beach
Hand in hand sunshine rays,
Beaming with the laughter of a song no longer sung.

Before beer fuelled riddles
Clenched fist
Forced love-carved nymphs,
To cower in silence from your once-strong arms.

Remind me of the time you loved me
And the monster was nothing but a dream
Or a fairy-tale.

Mama

They say I look like her
Mirror image
Opposite side of the same old rusty coin.

With a broken heart
She loved so hard
she created a miracle.
Blond hair, hazel eyes
Born 29 years and a month to the day apart
10 weeks early and she treated me like I was no less than perfect,
Just a little different from those other kids,
swinging from treetops so tall even the

Gods have trouble reaching them.
And yet, after all this time,
Through raging flame and flood,
She is the lifesaver,
The moral compass
That guides me home,
And reminds me that I belong.

Promise

In the chaos of this world
comes lightly shining
the glitter of what was promised,
my heart to yours.

As we leap over waterfalls,
Cascading hope
Hurtling towards a future that is not ours,
But should be protected all the same.
'Cause while they say life is short,
And we cannot guarantee
                    Tomorrow,
On this slippery slope of life,
There's no one else
                  With whom I'd rather be.

Heartbreak & Freedom

Are ones that love
Destined to tear apart those bonds
Shielded by insecurities and blinded
My selfishness.

Lose your way
Come find me.
Among the trees,
We shall play together
Like the innocents
We once were.

As it All Goes Black

Sorrow is a curtain that closes upon the
Best of people
At the worst times
In Life.
Gradually the curtain
Raises and you are to
Go on
Performing as though the lights never
Dimmed.

Rainbow

I picked a flower
I wandered through the trees
To find my way to you
But you had abandoned me.

Stand and Cry

Why don't I just stand and cry
For the little things, the sad things
The happy things.
For all that I've lost.

These frustrations weigh me down
And I am trapped in a cage
Of torment and rage.

Trapped

Darkness walks within the light
Hiding in the shadows.
You haunt me like there's
No tomorrow.
Tearing at the seams.

Let me be; let me live
in the positive of
The Future.

Of Love

Throw a party for me
With glittering lights.
Throw a party for me
Enjoy sweet delights.

Within the ballroom
I shall see
The one whom
I will marry

Beyond the masks
and behind the
capes I shall
Find my
Destined Fate.

Wildflowers

Ode to the wildflowers
In all their radiant shades
Petals falling like teardrops in lakes unexplored.
Blushing orange against the grey early morning
Shimmering beauty lay in green grass throwing purple on a cool autumn day.
Spring-filled blue defiant in red, against starry nights of undiscovered galaxies residing lightyears away.

Fireballs burning across glittering dew, sparks like a candle against the cold new moon.
Windswept dreams tell of promises unbroken,
Unsung songs on a cool breeze,
As we whisper goodnight among the trees to join oblivious sleep,
Fingers laced against the chill,
Pure and snow white like the first time we saw the light
Allowing two heartbeats to slow, and merge into one,
Creating the army against the darkness.

You

You ...
Don't know me but act as if you should.
You think
you are
above me
And aren't willing to give me the ladder.

You ...
Look at me
Like I'm a freak
What does that make you?

You ...
Make me cry
Strip me down
Naked
To reveal my insecurities
What right do you have?

Believe

Butterflies die after three days grace
with no one to mourn them but humanity.

Fragility exists in
Sights unseen
When there is no one looking out for me.

Rediscover the Saviour of
Life unknown.
Does He exist ...
or is it a cruel joke?

Fake (The Waltz)

Behind the mask
the tongue quickens
licking chafed lips
bruised from incessant kissing.

Behind the mask
her body is ruined
Stained
from a biting corset
Making her weep for innocence

But she takes a step forward
to join The Waltz
Vying for a glance
From a handsome Gent
Who can keep
her secure and comfortable
In the darkness of a controlling world?

Evil Surrenders

If the only way I can run
And escape this world where good is tarnished
And evil succeeds
Is to let evil override me and take me to a
Better place, I will.

Because then I can fly with the flock of doves
And soar like a wedge-tailed eagle,
Over the everlasting rainbow, following the sun,
To a place where people don't hurt
And evil surrenders.

Hide and Seek (A Game)

Are you there, my lucky friend?
Do you see me, from around the bend?
Watch me quiver and shake
Turn inside out.
I don't know
What this is all about.

Heal me
Make me sing
Shivering leaves
Do sway in trees
And I am lost without you
Come find me.

Minutes

The blackness of the searching skyline
Dawns on day.
Inviting those willing
In to the abyss of its temptations
Come what may.

The lives of others
Are turned upside down
Topsy-turvy, inside out.
Give me one chance
To figure this out.

One chance that's all I need
To bring together and stop the bleed

While watching the sunset over the horizon
I truly believe, nothing is all
And all is nothing.
Carry on fair moon,
Sleep well.

Sleeping Under Windowpanes

Sleeping under window panes
Staring out at sunsets
As the light fades
And blends into night
I wonder where I have been
Who I am
And where I come from
Are just fragments
Of who I was
Caught in this emotional
Turmoil of
Distress, heartache and love.

Please

I am a lone butterfly wandering free
I will die soon
Won't anyone save me?

Bruises

Innocence shattered ...
With the touch of a hand.
Deceiving apparitions ...
Playing torment with her mind.
Broken wings ...
Hinder this bird from flight.
Flowing blood ...
Scars cut deep.
Beautiful eyes ...
Fill with tears.
Static ...
Jumbles her thoughts.
Reality ...
Losing her grip.
Hidden away ...
Fragments of her true self.

Follow Me

A prayer for
Innocence
A prayer for
Joy
Eludes the
Devoted
of the Truth

Only the Destined
Has the Key
Only She will
Set Us Free.

Dreams

I hear voices
Calling my name
Telling me it's okay
And promising me
A simple life,
Though it may be.

I dream of sunny fields
And hope for sunny days
Waiting for someone
To wipe my tears away
And take a deep breath
To walk with me
Through this endless pain
And a dark, dark sea.

Talk to Me

Talk to me
As if I am your possession
Rather than your love
And I will walk away.

Serenity

It was an afternoon of quiet reflection,
A day of crystal blue.
Contemplation, reciprocation
Love and everything new.

Because everything is perfect
Everything is free.
Waves crash upon the surface light,
Drawing you near
And pulling you further out to sea
Giving me room to breathe.

Choke

Why do you not hate me?
Why do you love me?
I am not worthy of your love.
I am worthy only of your hate.
Shed your rose-coloured glasses.
SEE ME.
I am ugly. I am a disgrace. I am not worthy to breathe.

The Theory of Colour

Who decided that blood would be red,
drying chocolate brown on smudge-stained concrete?
DNA particles fuse with atoms to reveal
the make-up of me
pinpricks on rose thorns like smoke lost on the wind.

Rainbows dance upon the reflection of the sky
A shimmering, startling iridescent blue
But do the colour blind only see dreamscapes in greyscale?
The symphony that pulses through my untapped veins like rain
During heavy thunderstorms grows warm as a think of sunsets on the horizon,
Their lavender hues revealing hidden meaning to the monsters that lurk in the shadows of my mind.
And my pulse grows quicker as I wake from deep slumber to realise that I want to experience all the colour, even when my fractured heart will only paint in black and white.

Ancient Chapters (Red Herrings)

Speak in tongues
Then I might
Stand a chance of deciphering
The hieroglyphics of your words
And once again join
The path from which
I have been led astray
In this frail book of life.

Ambition

Fly on the wind
My sweet one
Take the chances
as they come.

This is your time
To Be
A spirit that is
Free
To bathe in the
Glory of the
Sun
and to you many
riches will come.

Perspective

Caught in the Web of your
Inner Turmoil
Like a spider seduces the fly,
You only see the night as it
Closes upon the day.

You don't see what I see,
The brilliant sunrise of your
Untapped Potential
As it struggles to shine
Behind the clouds of yesterday.

So walk with me a little while
We will not speak of the thoughts that
Trouble you but rather
Bask in the joy of
Beginning again
As we journey towards
A New Horizon.

Down

I am suffocating,
Sinking like an object that
does not float.
Confusion clouds my thoughts as I
Struggle to breathe.

Labyrinth

In the depth of the labyrinth
Surrounded by only fortified walls and the
Pit of your Despair,
The urge to surrender comes easy
As the storm clouds roll in and the
Dark of night
Takes over
The Day.

Just remember,
After every storm
There is a rainbow,
Weak though it may seem.

Sunlight will shine
Only if you let it.

I offer you my hand
And a friendly smile
Without judgement.

Together, we will journey
Through the maze of your Turmoil
And reach the other side.

Unknown

A mysterious place
    With a mysterious
    Face commands
        Others to
        Follow,

While lost
boys wander
    in desolate spaces
    searching for a loving
    Hand to guide them
    and a place to call
    Home.

Innocence

Happily, happily, happily
she rests in the
Dreaminess of sleep …
unfurling her hands
letting an occasional
cry wake her.

She does not realise
that we live in a world of
Chaos, destruction and mayhem.
All that matters is Mummy's milk and
her precious sleep.
So dream my little one,
I'll not disturb you.

There is plenty of time for that later.

In the Looking Glass

As I stand here
contemplating my Reflection
in a looking-glass too old to bear
I'm a shadow of the girl they once knew.

She looks at me through a
Curtain of black, hooded eyes and
Tear-stained cheeks.

She won't tell me her story,
that's asking too much
She would rather
Hide away
in the shadows of the former day.

I watch her crumble,
her walls broken
as I speak to her in a
Soft, complacent tone.
There are bruises on her chest,
Scars on her wrist.
Another child's innocence
Burned.

Home Truths and a Long Winding Road

Why do people have to change,
To grow up and live?

Why can't we all live in a perfect world?
Where everything turns out just the way we hoped!

Is life only about hurting people you love?
Is this the life I am supposed to live?
To go by the rules people make,
Even if it's not what their people want.

Does life set out to tell you home truths?
Or is it just a long winding road,
That never ends?

Communication Breakdown

Sometimes the writer in me takes a hold
And without a pen in my hand I cannot speak.
So I write and write and write
Until there is nothing left to say.

Held Captive

Held captive
By these thoughts and lies
An innocence that I despise.
I fumble through the darkness
With no pale light
To guide me
To the safety of the premise
Of my fragility.

Silent tears fall on deaf ears
My mouth is sewn shut
I try to scream
But all I hear
Is the silence of my pain.
A numbing transcendence into
Unanswered phones
And humming dial tones.

Nature

The wind is deep and cold and fresh
I weep for things I once
Possessed
And things I don't yet
Understand.

These bonds pull me down and
I fear ...
What is to become of me?

Leopards falter in the evening sun
Butterflies draw their wings
To a close and
Return to their cocoons.

Birds are hindered from flight
With broken wings
As insects mourn
The loss of
Sin.

Peace

Wounded soldiers
Lie in wait
On the path to freedom.

They have tried and failed
But should not feel ashamed.
They are heroes in our hearts.

Weary wives watch
Battle scenes on TV
And explain to
Four-year-old innocents
Why Daddy's missing Christmas.

Yes, Santa's still coming and
Rudolph too.
Whatever we do
We can't forget about you.

Escape

Fire, fire, burning bright.
Hush little one
dry your tears.

Run, run little one
Don't let them
See you.

You are destined for
More than this,
a future
Beyond me.

Blossom like the flower
You are meant to be.
Grow, fertilise, nourish
I cannot
Provide for you.
        Be better than me.
        Be yourself.

Someday

Someday
I will stand on my
Own
instead of
Crawl
With others
who do not recognise my potential.

Someday I will be
Free to live
Without Fear
Of prying eyes
and a cynical attitude.

Poetry in Motion

Behind her eyes lie a simile,
sparkling in its knowing way.
Her lips are a metaphor for a brand-new day.
Her voice is a song,
Calming through and through
The promise of tomorrow, a new chapter
in this book of life
Presents itself in words unspoken and sentences unbidden.

The fragment of the clause, a semi-colon scribbled for pause.
Remove the mask and you will read the misremembered lyric you've been searching for
The memory of a fear unafraid of the spotlight
Because what was once golden
Does not always remain
As she speaks the words I fear to say.

Nostalgia

On days like this,
when memory is not far
from the surface,
I am grateful for the time I had
With you.

I can hear it,
the sounds of laughter,
and your voice
something I thought I'd forgotten.
Those melodic sounds.

Close my eyes and
I can almost touch you,
Your tissue-like skin all mottled in places,
The red, white, and deep blue of veins
Overworked.

I miss you.

Home

In the cacophony of household noise,
Comes a silence both comforting and
Restorative.

Amid the snippets of conversation,
discussions of what to do next week,
or the faraway laughter of neighbours,
comes the calming wind whistling through the trees
an explanation of connection, unity and what it all means.

The rustle of papers, a bird singing, clanging of pans and cutlery
Shuffling footsteps of family preparing lunch,
all part of the routine that is daily life,
Sparking
beauty in the mundane.

The Fires

The warning came in
Shades of Grey
In the morning light
Mother Nature called
To the Defenceless
And their prey.

'It's time for renewal,
Time for new life.'

So renew yourself
And begin again.
Start over my darling friends
Call on the wind
And I will look after you.
Because it's for my children,
I will choose.

Riot

A pessimistic nobody shouting about how the world is ending
Hands flailing with emotion
Passes for news for those hung up on the
                                          FAKE,

Fire burning glass ceilings,
Shattering hearts like memory.

The town crier calls for peace where there is none,
The wounded voices uniting as one
over bruises and scars of the past,
Leaving the ashes of a future once pure
For those who have yet to come.

Why?

Why do raindrops fall like revealing tears of our emotions?
Why do people have to die and never be replaced?

Why do we have to be hurt, by people we thought cared
Leaving scars that may never be healed.

There is one question that I would like answered
And that is ...
Why?

Drowning

Water lilies gather upon the ocean's surface,
A remnant of the war that rages beneath.
On Neptune's order
A lover is lost upon frail seas as nymphs bear witness to the
world
That crushes my
Too fragile heart.

Dancer

If I could dance
I'd be a butterfly,
Flitting from flower to flower.

I'd spread my wings and arch my back
Taller and straighter than ever before.

I'd extend upon my tip toes,
Leaping,
jumping,
twirling,
twisting
pirouetting my way around you.

If I could dance,
I'd finally be free.

Stalker

It's summer and I walk until the sun sets,
follow the sparkling dawn as night meets the horizon,
footsteps so light behind you I may as well be your shadow.
watch from across the street as you get your coffee from our favourite shop.
(caramel vanilla latte, you might as well be drinking sugar).
I seize the day as you did the night,
our new arrangement –
or whatever you want to call it –
because even though there is no longer an us,
I am still half you half me,
Lost in this split personality,
And for now,
That is OK.

Midnight Conversations (Sleeping Dogs Lie)

In the still of the night
Dogs bark in
Language unheard by human counterparts.

Reminiscing those days long ago
Ancestors running free
When they were kings of the forest,
And everyone fell on bended knee.

Midnight strikes,
The clock has struck
And their silence must return.

Time is golden,
Curse forgotten
Yet still the candle burns.

Prisoner

What became of Freedom who
called himself my Own?
Now I sit here in chains
shackled to the floor.

These bars constrict and
choke my voice.
I've lost the will to fight
and I don't cry lonesome anymore.

For the tears are all dry
There is chaos in the meaning
When I sleep at night
I am no longer dreaming.

Freedom
Rescue me from my thoughts
There are monsters under the bed,
and I can't even talk.

                                              The static is so loud.

I've Been Thinking

I've been thinking
About how you said you love me
But do not want
To see me follow dreams
Or a road of cotton candy.

Sorry for Your Loss

My black petals drip like blood on
crisp white hospital sheets as wives mourn the loss of you.

I am the comforting hand that guides you,
Reminds you of loved ones embraces
When words are not enough.

I witness too much of this world
Before I begin to wither and grow anew
Like a phoenix from the ashes.

The hospital beds, endless tears and joyful smiles
Pain me
I know that time is fleeting,
And one day soon, we will meet again,
In life's inevitable end.

Isolation

I don't remember your jokes,
but I know how I felt when you told them;
that warm embrace like hot chocolate in
mid-winter.
This memory holds me softly at night,
transcending time and distance,
reminding me that this too shall pass and
tomorrow
I am one day closer to
Seeing you again.

Destiny in Black and White

I see a man, in a black and white photo.
He is dressed formally, in a tie, jacket and shirt.
His hair is brushed back neatly
He isn't smiling but you can see the mystery in his eyes
And it's funny.

I see a woman in a black and white photo,
She is dressed in an old-fashioned blouse and has
a brooch on.
She wears no other jewellery.
Her hair is short and kind of fly-away.
She is smiling pleasantly for the camera.
But you can see the amusement in her eyes.

Who knew that one day Fate would bring these two together, forever?
And they thought they could love others but how is that possible
When they are so obviously right for one another?
The mystery in the man's eyes cleared when he met her.

CPSIA information can be obtained
at www.ICGtesting.com
Printed in the USA
BVHW042345050721
611171BV00012B/2012